more than

101 ways

to know you're a medical writer

Edited by Donna Miceli

Editorial Rx Press

This book includes content generously donated by medical writers
and communicators. Permission to reuse this material will be
granted to all contributors upon request.

"Applied Knowledge: Medical Writing vs. Pie Baking" and "Applied
Knowledge: Medical Writing vs. the Renal System" were provided by
Barbara Snyder, MA, and is published with permission by Ms. Snyder,
who retains copyright for these materials.

A selection adapted from Chapter 5 of *Elements of Medical Terminology*
by Barbara Gastel, MD, MPH, "Some Amusing Terms Coined by AMWA
Workshop Attendees," is reprinted with permission. American Medical
Writers Association, Rockville, MD, retains copyright for this material.

All requests for use and reuse of all other material published in this
book should be directed to the book's editor c/o Editorial Rx Press,
P.O. Box 794, Orange Park, FL 32067. Permission must be granted
by the editor for the use and reuse of this text.

A compilation of content reflective of the professional lives of
medical writers and communicators

Cover and book design by Biographics (www.biographicsweb.com)

Editorial Rx Press, Registered Office:
P.O. Box 794
Orange Park, FL 32067
United States
www.editorialrxpress.com
info@editorialrxpress.com

First Editorial Rx Press printing Fall/Winter 2010

10 9 8 7 6 5 4 3 2 1

Library of Congress Cataloging in Publication Data

Miceli, Donna, 1940- --editor
More Than 101 Ways to Know You're a Medical Writer;
Edited by Donna Miceli
Foreword by Michele Vivirito

ISBN: 978-0-9799274-8-5
1. Medical writing—humor
2. Medical writing—and freelance life
3. Compilation—medical communicators
4. Non-fiction—medical writing, general

Dedication

In memory of my husband Art, whose love
and support made all things possible.

Contents

Contents

From the Editor

The seed for this book was planted during the 2007 American Medical Writers Association (AMWA) Annual Conference in Atlanta when I attended a "How-to Session" on using humor in health writing led by Neil Shulman, MD. Dr Shulman, recipient of AMWA's 2006 Alvarez Award, is a physician and author who is best known for the book "Doc Hollywood," which was made into a 1991 movie starring Michael J. Fox. He is also famous for using humor to teach about serious medical issues. During his presentation, Dr Shulman mentioned a book he'd written entitled "*101 Ways to Know You're a Nurse.*" That immediately commanded my attention and I glanced at Michele Vivirito, who was moderating the session. I could tell she was thinking the same thing I was: Wouldn't it be great if we could come up with 101 ways to know you're a medical writer? Michele and I talked about it after the session, and I decided to get AMWA members involved by incorporating the idea into the Creative

Readings session, for which I was the moderator, at the 2008 Annual Conference in St. Louis.

I introduced the project in the pre-conference publicity for the Creative Readings session, inviting members to bring their ideas to the session, or e-mail them to me prior to the conference, and promising to share some of them during the session. Much to my surprise, within minutes of when the "AMWA Update" containing this information was e-mailed to members, I started receiving responses to my request. By the time the St. Louis conference ended, I had received approximately 70 contributions. Hoping to increase that number to 101, after I returned home from the St. Louis conference, I sent a post to the AMWA Freelance Listserve asking for suggestions on "ways to know you're a *freelance* medical writer." Once again the response was immediate and overwhelming. Never underestimate the enthusiasm and creativity of AMWA members!

From the beginning, I had hoped to find a way to share the results of this creative endeavor with all AMWA members, but hadn't given much serious thought to what might be the best way to do that. I didn't have to wonder for long. Within a few days of when I first announced the project, fellow

AMWA member Deb Whippen, Publisher and Editor of Editorial Rx, Inc. and its publishing subsidiary Editorial Rx Press, expressed interest in publishing the results for us. We had some initial discussions about it, but, before we had a chance to move ahead, my husband became seriously ill and I put everything aside to care for him.

It has taken longer than planned, but we hope you'll be pleased with the results and agree that it is worth the wait.

– Donna Miceli, Editor

Contributors

This book would not be possible without the creative and enthusiastic contributions of the following medical writers and AMWA members.

Lanie Adamson	Emma Hitt
Peter Aitken	Kristie Holt
Cynthia Arnold	Keven Kehres
Heather Banks	Kathleen Kite-Powell
Lois Baker	Mary King
Genevieve Belfiglio	Gretchen M. Longcore
Julie Kay Beyrer	Dawn Maxemow
Kim Berman	Jeanne McAdara-Berkowitz
Alisa Bonsignore	Kristen Phiel
Rebecca Bowes	Barbara Rinehart
Deb Bruce	Caitlin Rothermel
Leslie Charles	Meredith Rogers
Jim Cozzarin	Gayle Scott
Renee Cohen	Barbara Snyder
Bruce B. Dan	Peter Steinberg
Dan Croft	Rebecca Stadolnik
Debbie Due	Nancy Tennent
Nancy Faass	Rebecca Teaff
Jayne G	Cindy Van Dijk
Debra Gordon	Ann Volk
Carol Green	Alan Wachter
Elyse Dubno Grusky	Deb Whippen
Neil R. Grobman	Bruce Wilson
Karen Harrop	Marjorie Winters

Foreword

Those who tickle themselves may laugh when they please.

German proverb

Do you know medical writers who take themselves too seriously? I do. In fact, I'm one of them! Medical writing is a serious business. After all, we write about life-and-death issues every day. We are usually the ones called on to explain worrisome diagnoses to friends and family members. But to be effective in our work, we must keep a sense of humor about it.

When I read this book in draft form, my reaction, just a couple of times, was "I don't get it." When I thought about it more carefully, I realized that I was missing the absurdity in a clearly absurd situation. So, I relaxed and allowed myself to be teased, even tickled. As you read these contributions of fellow medical writers, I suggest that you relax, stop editing, and come up with your own ways to know you're a medical writer. Then you'll be in the enviable position of tickling yourself and having a good laugh, perhaps when you need it most.

And remember, you need a good laugh very badly if you find yourself saying (as I did):

You know you're a medical writer when your reaction to this book, just a couple of times, is: "What's so funny about that?"

– Michele Vivirito

Introduction

What is a medical writer? We've all heard that question more times than we can count. According to information on the American Medical Writers Association (AMWA) Web site, "Medical communicators write, edit, or develop material about medicine and health." Although that is a concise and accurate definition, it doesn't begin to convey the extent of what AMWA members do or the diversity of our membership. And it is precisely that diversity that makes it so difficult to accurately convey what a medical writer/communicator is.

Some of us are doctors, dentists, veterinarians, nurses, or PharmDs who write journal articles, books, regulatory documents, and continuing medical education programs. Some of us are journalists who write news articles, patient information brochures, sales training manuals, and Web content; and help doctors, dentists, veterinarians, nurses and PharmDs write journal articles and books. Some of us are marketing experts who write sales materials for the pharmaceutical industry and medical device companies. Some of us are English majors who specialize in editing medical/scientific material others have written, and maybe do some writing on the side. Some of us are educators who teach others about medical/technical communication.

Although there are many differences in what we do as medical communicators, we share common experiences, like the ones in this book, that are uniquely associated with our chosen profession. We know we are medical writers when...

The Life of a Medical Writer

Benefits

You know you're a medical writer when...

You can ask a researcher a question
that includes the word "penis"
without blushing.

***

You're trying to keep a lot of people,
including yourself, well hydrated.

***

You have the most wonderful,
fascinating colleagues
you've ever met.

Benefits

You know you're a medical writer when...

You actually read the package inserts
enclosed with your prescriptions;
and then, without thinking,
start trying to verify the data.

***

One of your little joys is figuring out
how to explain complex science in a
sound bite that the guy at the corner
store can understand.

***

You leave an AMWA Conference with
a full brain, from all the knowledge
you gained, and a full heart, from all
the wonderful people you met.

Drawbacks

You know you're a medical writer when...

You've just read an article on
myocardial infarction and notice
pain in your left arm.

***

You've heard "The Health Authority
has a 48-hour turnaround time"
for the third time in a month.

***

You can't read the local paper
without gritting your teeth
over the bad grammar.

Drawbacks

You know you're a medical writer when...

The grammatical errors of the
Presidential candidates, such as
"because of the fact that,"
really bother you.

***

You can't attend a lecture
without critiquing the slides.

***

You're at a social gathering and
friends say, "Tell me again
what it is you do."

Family and Friends

You know you're a medical writer when...

Your 4 year old refuses to get a
face painting at the county fair, claiming
"You could get Hepatitis C from tattoos."

***

You accompany your spouse to a doctor's
appointment and speak more medical
jargon than the resident doing the
work-up, and find yourself watching
the neurology testing and running a
diagnosis chart in your head.

***

Friends and family members call
you for medical advice before
contacting their physician.

Family and Friends

You know you're a medical writer when...

Your child's preschool teacher
explains to the class that she has
a baby growing in her belly, and
your child remarks, "That's unusual,
most babies grow in the uterus."

***

Your sister tells you about a friend
who is suffering from some rare
disease and asks you to do some
research to find out more about it.

Family and Friends

You know you're a medical writer when...

You tell your friends and family members
to, "Get a second opinion."

***

Your significant other reads your
work when he/she has trouble
falling asleep.

***

Your Mom introduces you as
"a writer but not like Danielle Steele."

***

A friend asks, "Would you read this
stuff if you didn't write this stuff?"

Habits

You know you're a medical writer when...

You sneeze into the crook of your elbow.

***

You like to avoid shaking hands.

***

You hear yourself saying words like "STAT" in regular conversation.

***

You look at license plates and see not randomly generated nonsensical combinations of letters, but medical acronyms.

Habits

You know you're a medical writer when...

You read medical journals just for fun.

***

The first thing you do each day is check the "Health" pages of the *Wall Street Journal*.

***

The subject of your last e-mail of the day begins with "Fifth final sign-off..."

***

You discuss bovine viral diarrhea over lunch.

Habits

You know you're a medical writer when...

You look up a medical term definition in *Dorland's* and then check it in *Stedman's*.

***

You have Poison Control on speed dial, just because they're so darn interesting to talk to.

***

You accidentally use phrases like "prospectively showed"; "thus, in summary"; and "concomitantly" in daily conversation, and you really aren't trying to show off.

How Do I Explain?

You know you're a medical writer when...

The person you're talking with looks confused and doesn't quite know what to say after you respond to their question about what you do for a living.

***

The New England Journal of Medicine is your favorite magazine.

***

You get excited about well-designed medical textbooks.

How Do I Explain?

You know you're a medical writer when...

You'd rather write a proposal to
do research than
actually do the research.

***

Your bible is the
AMA Manual of Style.

***

You have a serious e-mail
discussion about cat sphincters
with your client.

How Do I Explain?

You know you're a medical writer when...

You explain that you are not a medical
transcriptionist to those who
think you are when you
say 'medical writer.'

***

You are getting good at
describing the difference
between a 'medical writer'
and a 'ghost writer.'

***

It matters how many AMWA pins and
ribbons you can wear during the
national AMWA Annual Conference.

How Medical Writing Changes Me

You know you're a medical writer when...

You believe that "be well" is among the most important and meaningful things you can say to someone.

***

A friend tells you that she/he is sick and you ask, "What's the system, organ, class, and preferred term."

***

You get a form asking you to check male or female under the heading SEX and you cross the heading out and write in GENDER.

You know you're a medical writer when...

You get excited about distilling the content of a clinical study or medical journal article into language a lay audience can understand, when most "normal" people would run for the hills if they had to do it.

***

You wonder if you should get your doctorate just to blend in.

***

You have a visceral reaction when seeing the word "significant" that has no P value with it.

***

You've used the ICH-E3 guidelines as light bedtime reading.

You know you're a medical writer when...

Your favorite "mysteries" are real-life medical mysteries, emerging pathogens, and science that defies logic.

***

You check the acknowledgments in journal articles you read just to make sure the writers are mentioned—and to see if you know them.

***

You are finally able to explain your job in one sentence, and people seem to "get" what it is you do.

Medical Advice

You know you're a medical writer when...

You ask your physician for drugs
by chemical compound rather
than brand name.

***

If you must enter the hospital as a
patient, you bring a sign to place
above your bed that reads:
If you haven't washed your hands,
don't even think about touching me.

***

You begin sentences by saying,
"I'm not a doctor, BUT..."

You know you're a medical writer when...

While waiting in line at the grocery
store or post office, you are tempted
to tell the person in front of you
that they seem to have symptoms
of a condition you wrote about recently.

***

Your family doctor and dentist
speak to you as if you were
a professional medical colleague.

***

After writing an article about
nosocomial infections, you start
paying attention to your
doctor's tie and shirt cuffs.

You know you're a medical writer when...

You tell your doctor his/her
diagnosis is wrong.

***

You ask your doctor if he/she's
read a recent journal article
in his/her specialty.

***

You're choosing a new physician,
and you look up his/her
publications and credentials.

You know you're a medical writer when...

You find yourself editing the
educational materials on display
in your doctor's office.

***

You become convinced that you have
whatever disease you're writing about,
which really sucks when you're in a
middle of a 30-slide deck on
overactive bladder.

***

You find yourself critiquing the
paragraph structure of patient
brochures in the waiting room
at the doctor's office.

Popular Culture

You know you're a medical writer when...

You're aware of the latest advance in liquid-crystal diagnostics, but don't know who was voted out last night on "Dancing with the Stars."

***

You already know about the obscure illnesses featured on "Grey's Anatomy" and find yourself critiquing how they are presented.

***

You analyze the patient's vital signs and symptoms, and determine the correct diagnosis 15 minutes before "House" does.

You know you're a medical writer when...

Your conversations with friends about your favorite prime-time medical show focus less on the characters' romantic lives and more on the medical inaccuracies.

***

You begin mindlessly correcting the pronunciation of the reporters on the 6 o'clock news.

***

You've successfully figured out the patient's illness on "Mystery Diagnosis" because you wrote a review article on the topic the previous week.

You know you're a medical writer when...

You think a song you hear
on the radio would make
a great health "ditty."

* * *

You can't help critiquing
pharmaceutical ads to anyone in
your living room who will listen.

Technology

You know you're a medical writer when...

You procrastinate by responding to
the AMWA listserves.

***

You join all the social networks on
the Internet, even though you have
absolutely no clue about what
they are and how they work.

***

If someone screamed "End Note!"
while pulling out their hair,
you would understand.

You know you're a medical writer when...

You regularly run a word search
for "trail" to clean documents
of "clinical trails."

***

A medical abbreviations website
is first on your favorites list.

***

You think the German photographic
rendition of the English word "science"
spelled out by manipulating single
strands of DNA, is the coolest thing,
and worthy of a place on your
workplace wall.

Words and Language

You know you're a medical writer when...

You can't help but look for errors
in grammar or sentence structure
in everything you read.

***

You get emotional over the
issue of verb agreement
with the word "data."

***

Every time you see the word
"judgment" written somewhere,
you look closely to see that it
doesn't have another "e" in it.

You know you're a medical writer when...

You change everyone's "which" to the more correct "that"; or visa versa.

***

You misread "antispam" as "anitspasm."

***

You find yourself typing "patients" when you mean "patience," or "medication" when you mean "meditation."

***

You like saying "umlaut" and spelling out SAS just for the heck of it.

You know you're a medical writer when...

You inadvertently ask the supermarket manager where you can find the vanilla abstract.

***

You spend a 45-minute bus trip talking about punctuation.

***

You can't help laughing when, while rewriting colonscopy instructions for a clinic, you refer to the reader as "the end user"—no pun intended.

***

The word "timeline" is your personal swear word.

Work Issues

You know you're a medical writer when...

While updating files about some common diseases, you see nothing wrong in hollering office-to-office to another writer: "Have you got syphilis?" And you barely blink when he responds: "No, I gave it to Peggy."

* * *

Your clinical program planning meetings take up more of your time than writing your documents.

You know you're a medical writer when...

You've learned that "data base lock"
means you'll be eating dinner
in your office for the next month.

***

You write your job title on your annual
performance evaluation as "Sr. miracle
writer" and don't bat an eye.

The Freelance Life

Benefits

You know you're a freelance medical writer when...

You are looking out the window of your office and decide to take a stroll in the beautiful sunshine despite having a tight project deadline.

***

You enjoy a great glass of wine in the middle of the day.

***

You take a break from writing to reapply sunscreen.

Benefits

You know you're a freelance medical writer when...

You don't get out of your
pajamas before noon.

***

You organize your work wardrobe by
"work jammies" and "play jammies."

***

You go to work in your "bunny slippers."

***

The Fedex driver no longer looks
embarrassed when you answer
the door in your bathrobe.

***

You're on a first name basis with
the employees at the coffee shop.

Benefits

You know you're a freelance medical writer when...

You are editing an abstract for the American College of Surgeons conference on your iPhone while bathing two children.

***

Multitasking means folding the laundry while listening in on a call that your client insists you participate in just in case a medical question your client can't answer is asked.

***

You can secure new business while on vacation and enjoying Friday afternoon cocktail hour.

Drawbacks

You know you're a freelance medical writer when...

You don't realize how little human contact you have until you become the person who talks everyone's ear off at a party.

***

You seem to "lose" your business card everywhere you go.

***

You begin arguing with yourself about the validity of a clinical study's results and/or the methods used to arrive at them.

***

You have no idea what most of your clients actually look like, but can easily recognize their voices.

Drawbacks

You know you're a freelance medical writer when...

You consider the walk to the mailbox to be a big event in your day.

***

You have to stop yourself from viewing the Web site for Varmint Hunter instead of finishing the current project.

***

Every day you think you have a different disease, depending on what you are writing about.

Work Issues

You know you're a freelance medical writer when...

You receive a call on Thursday about a project that is due the following Monday and say, "Yes, I can do it."

***

You review photos of a cadaver dissection while eating lunch.

***

You send Christmas gifts to people you never met.

Work Issues

You know you're a freelance medical writer when...

At the beginning of the month, you find yourself reviewing which of the accounts receivables did not arrive yet.

***

Medical writers who agree to extremely low rates cause you emotional pain.

***

Your file of clippings about medicine is taking over your filing cabinet.

Pets and Animals

You know you're a freelance medical writer when...

Your cat knows better than to jump on your lap while you're writing.

***

You mumble health advice to your chickens while servicing their coop.

***

You spend more time talking to your dogs than with other human beings.

***

You've trained your parrot to supply the "right word" when you're stumped.

Family

You know you're a freelance medical writer when...

You ask your 11-year-old son to make copies of references from a textbook, and don't even consider the fact that the project is on breast reconstruction.

***

Your college-aged daughter goes in your office to call a friend and you hear her saying, "I'm in my Mother's office and there are pictures of penises all over the floor."

***

Your kids see your office is empty and assume you're not home without even bothering to look for you elsewhere in the house.

Family

You know you're a freelance medical writer when...

You realize you forgot to take down the photos of breast reconstruction before allowing your visiting teenage nephews to sleep in your office.

***

Your project white board reads: "Major depressive disorder briefs"; "Chronic pain article"; "Sexuality questions"; "Opioid-induced constipation monograph"; and "Venous thromboembolism needs analysis."

Appendix

Editor's Note

After joining AMWA—and especially after attending your first AMWA Annual Conference—it quickly becomes clear that our members are far more than just talented, dedicated medical writers and editors. As a group, we seem to have more than our share of gifted, individuals with a wide range of creative interests. If you need proof, just look at the list of topics for the "Coffee and Dessert Klatches" or attend one of the "Creative Readings" sessions at the conference. Better yet, take time to read the samples of AMWA member creativity included in this Appendix.

As mentioned in the Introduction, one of the challenges we face in our chosen profession is trying to explain exactly what it is we do. Using a table format—an important communication tool for all medical/technical writers—Barbara Snyder has tackled that challenge in two unique, but distinctly different, ways. Who would have guessed that medical writing and pie baking had so much in common?

Members who have taken Dr Barbara Gastel's medical terminology workshop will be familiar with the assignment to coin their own medical terms using the knowledge gained in the workshop. We thank Dr Gastel, and AMWA, for allowing us to share this excerpt from Chapter 5 of the newly released self-study module *Elements of Medical Terminology*.

I said it before, but it's worth repeating: Never underestimate the enthusiasm and creativity of AMWA members!

Applied Knowledge:
Medical Writing vs. Pie Baking

By Barbara Snyder, MA

Lesson Learned	Pies	Regulatory Submissions
Experience helps (also known as "practice makes perfect")	It sometimes takes years to learn to make really good pie-crust, but you'll get better at it each time you try	Each time through the process of writing regulatory documents is easier than the last, as we learn what works best
New equipment can increase efficiency, even if it takes a while to learn to use it properly	An apple peeler/corer/slicer can make your job easier	Increased electronic capability (eg, reviewer annotations on PDF files rather than on paper copies) makes our job easier in the long run
Some imperfection is expected–it won't affect the final product	A slightly lop-sided crust will taste just as good as a perfect one	We must truly understand what's "good enough" and make only value-added changes
Proper timing and priority calls are important	Bananas spoil before apples– use the bananas first	Understand critical chain sequencing– "just in time" is better than "as soon as possible" when you have multiple projects

Lesson Learned	Pies	Regulatory Submissions
Best ingredients = best product	Don't use lard when the recipe calls for butter	There's no substitute for good data
Things can get messy when the fruit isn't perfect, but that doesn't necessarily preclude a good final product	Cut out the bruises, then make sure you have enough good apple to continue	Thoroughly explore unexpected findings– subgroup analyses may help
Less effort some-times produces a better result	An overworked crust will be tough	Don't over-analyze and over-interpret the data
Follow the recipe	Measure your ingredients carefully and add them in the correct order	Follow the guidelines (eg, ICH Common Technical Document)
Always double-check your work	Ask yourself, "Was that 1 cup flour and 2 of sugar or 2 cups flour and 1 of sugar?"	Perform a quality-control check on every document
When in doubt, ask	Call Mom	Talk to your regulatory agency reviewer(s)
The kitchen is hottest just before the final product is complete	Self-explanatory!	Self-explanatory!

Applied Knowledge:
Medical Writing vs. the Renal System

By Barbara Snyder, MA

Renal System	Pharmaceutical Company
Anatomical part/Responsibility	**Company role/Responsibility**
Heart → Indiscriminately pumps the blood	**Chief Executive Officer** → Pumps dollars and demands through the system. Doesn't care how something gets done, as long as it doesn't produce a drag on the CEO
Renal artery (Big Red) → Carries the blood from the heart to the kidney	**Vice President** → (renal artery) commits to some deadline or partner contract and delegates all the subsequent required planning and execution because he/she is too big to actually get into the working units **Directors** (large blood vessels) → delegates to Project Leaders **Project Leader** (smaller blood vessel) → delegates to Project Team **Project Team** (capillaries) → does the work (nobody left to delegate to)
Lungs → Oxygenates the blood, then works with the kidneys to set and maintain physiological pH (7.4)	**Regulatory Affairs Dept** → Negotiates with global agencies, then has very little to do with the submission until the writers and project team are done with most of the other work

Renal System	Pharmaceutical Company
Anatomical part/Responsibility	Company role/Responsibility
Proximal tubule → Sends the body the good stuff it needs (eg, glucose, salt, amino acids) after filtering out the bad stuff	**Medical Writer** → Does 70% of the nephron's work; Knows and gives the body (the larger organization) exactly what it needs; Not only does its own job, but also identifies potentially serious issues that nobody else has identified (eg, deciding whether the pH is in the right range) and actually does something about it (eg, regulates bicarbonate)
Loop of Henle → Further filters the blood, but its biggest accomplishment is transporting sodium against a high concentration to establish a hypertonic environment	**Editor** → Highly specialized; Does about 30% of the work; Can make the entire project team change directions in a hairpin-turn-like manner
Counter-current mechanism → Concentrates the urine by repeatedly exchanging solutes between the 2 sides of the Loop of Henle	**Author/editor exchanges** → This process distills documents into a highly concentrated end product
Juxtaglomerular apparatus → Where the fluid enters the distal tubule; Releases prostaglandins if the salt level isn't high enough.	**Quality control auditor** → Last quality check before the final review. Has connections with internal management (afferent arterioles) and the outside (efferent arterioles)

Renal System	Pharmaceutical Company
Anatomical part/Responsibility	**Company role/Responsibility**
Distal tubule → Final filtration structure before the collecting tube.	**Reviewer** → Doesn't have much to do if the proximal tubule (writers) and Loop of Henle (editors) have done their jobs, but is necessary to move stuff through the process
Urea → Waste product that results when there's not enough pressure to push the fluid through the tubules.	**Unwanted / unneeded reviewer comments** → Every time the reviewers read a document, they have more comments and create more rework; Only when pressured by a deadline or by orders from upper management does this stop
Collecting duct → Receives and combines the input from several nephrons	**Publishing** → Gathers all the documents from the various writers to compile the submission
Anti-diuretic hormone → Hormone released by the pituitary gland in response to dehydration	**Investigator's comments** → Can result in a concentration or dilution of meaning in a document or submission
Renin-angiotension system → Increases blood pressure	**FDA** → Increases blood pressure

Some Amusing Terms Coined by AMWA Workshop Attendees[1]

By Barbara Gastel, MD, MPH

In the live version of the AMWA medical-terminology workshop, the homework includes coining a medical term of one's own and providing a definition. To do so, participants can both use course materials and consult other resources, such as a medical dictionary and medical-terminology Web sites. This exercise induces participants to become better acquainted with components of medical terms, and it helps give a feel for how medical terms are constructed. And for those participants who wish to coin humorous medical terms, the exercise provides a chance to display their wit.

At the workshop, each participant receives a list of all the terms and definitions. Participants vote, by secret ballot, on which term they think is best. The coiners of the most popular terms receive small prizes.

---

[1] from Gastel B, *Elements of Medical Terminology*. American Medical Writers Association, 2010, Rockville, MD

To end this book with some lighthearted review, and with glimpses of some additional word components out there, here are some favorite definitions from over the years. Some have been slightly edited. Thanks to the now-anonymous participants who submitted these definitions.

- akinophilia: the love of not moving
- amourarrhythmia: the irregular heart rhythm resulting from being in love
- androgenetic amaurosis (male-pattern blindness): the inability, more prominent in men, but also occurring in girls and young women, to see items they are searching for even when they are in plain view!
- bradymentosis: slow mind
- cephalosclerograph: an instrument that measures the hardness of the head
- hydrophobia: fear of sweating
- hypercyanoblepharosis: too much blue eye shadow
- hyperdynamic ectorectal pneumatogenesis (HEP): a condition characterized by overactivity in the production in release of gases from the rectum
- hypermalapedostomatisis: state of excessive bad-mouthing by a child
- hyperosteocephalopathy: condition characterized by excessively thick skull

- hypojocularosis: abnormally low sense of humor
- labiomegaly: enlargement of the lips (whether natural or artificial)
- macropodologist: one who studies large feet
- micropizzalatus: small pizza on the side
- neurofrenetic: in a state in which one's last nerve is being frazzled
- polygnosia gravis: severe "information overload": a stressful condition caused by a barrage of constant "knowledge"/info in daily work
- postmenopausal mammamegaly: big breasts after menopause
- pseudocerebromegaly: an unwarranted belief in the size (importance) of one's brain
- rhinocarcinophobia: an abnormal fear of nose cancer
- rhinophage: something that eats noses
- somnigenesis felinus: the ability of cats to induce sleep in nearby humans (by giving of "snooze rays")
- tachyglossal: pertaining to having a quick tongue
- ultrahypnophilia: excessive love of sleep

If you have ultrahypnophilia, perhaps take a nap before proceeding.

Editor Bio

Donna Miceli, a native of Western New York State, earned a BS in journalism and speech from Syracuse University. She has been a freelance medical writer for more than 20 years. Her prior work experience includes writing a weekly newspaper column, doing freelance copywriting for small advertising agencies, and serving as Assistant Director of Public Relations for a large hospital in Buffalo, NY. An active member of AMWA since 1989, when she joined the Delaware Valley Chapter, Donna served on  a variety of committees at the national level and moderated or chaired Annual Conference sessions, including the Creative Reading session, which she chaired for several years. She also authored a chapter section in *Essays for Biomedical Communicators: Volume 2 of Selected AMWA Workshops: A Practical Guide for Writers, Editors, and Presenters of Health Science Information*.* Donna, who was elected an AMWA Fellow in 2007, has been a member of the AMWA Executive Committee since 2008. She was recently named Administrator for Publications. Currently a member of the AMWA Florida Chapter, Donna lives in Ft. Myers and considers herself "semi-retired."

*Witte FM and Taylor ND (eds). American Medical Writers Association, Bethesda, MD, 1997